ISAs
Made
Easy

An Investors Guide to
Individual Savings
Accounts

Stefan Bernstein

With John Lyons & Eric Clarkson

TAKE THAT LTD.

Take That Ltd.
P.O.Box 200
Harrogate
HG1 2YR
England
Fax: 01423-526035
Email: sales@takethat.co.uk
http://www.takethat.co.uk/Fbooks.htm

You should take independent financial advice before acting on material contained in this book.

ISBN 1-873668-61-9

Contents

Introduction

The ISA, or Individual Savings Account, is a very significant development in the field of personal financial planning and the general investment market. Even if it offered no benefits whatsoever in itself, the fact that it signals the end for PEPs and TESSAs, is in itself extremely important. Not only that, but with successive Governments tinkering with pensions and state benefits, it is conceivable that the ISA could become the core financial planning instrument for many people. The ISA should not be ignored, and this book is intended to help you put it in the context of your own savings and the various other financial instruments that are available.

It is impossible to guess at this stage how widespread the use of ISAs will become, or how highly they will be developed. It is, however, significant to note that money under-management in personal equity plans (PEPs) is now estimated at £77.5 billion, and the amount of dealing commission and management fees that this generates for the investment world is considerable. Also, the number of people who hold PEPs, and who may be relying upon them to repay mortgages, boost retirement income, help with school fees, or simply pay for a specific need such as a new car or holiday, is also estimated at over three million with 15.5 million plans in existence. Given this level of diversified interest in PEPs, it is likely that considerable self-interest will be brought to bear on ISAs, which should help them become a success.

What also gives the ISA added significance, is that it is the first financial instrument created by New Labour. As such, you can expect it to be around for several years, because the loss of face involved if it were to be shelved would be considerable. Indeed, it would be political suicide to allow it to become another "poll tax", whereby millions are spent in producing a strategy that is discontinued a few years down the line due to imperfections.

That is not to say of course that it will not be developed and altered as time goes by. Already in the early stages of its development, the investment world (committees of private investors, treasury officials and politicians along with consumer organisations and the Inland Revenue) have all had their say on how the original suggestions and structure were not suitable. Accordingly, we already have a reasonably refined instrument, but one which will undoubtedly require more attention once it reaches the real acid test of the consumer.

It would be easy to ignore the ISA, (although not perhaps the intensive marketing that goes with it), but this is likely to be a mistake. If you consider what happened with personal equity plans, those who recognised their value from the start now have significant portfolios of entirely tax-free gains and income. It is a sobering thought, but if over the last twelve years a husband and wife had each saved £25 a week into a tax-free PEP, rather than a taxable account, then the non-taxable fund would be 20% bigger.

Moreover, because the PEP fund can give tax-free income, then even at today's tax rates the effective spendable income from the tax-free portfolio would be 84% higher than that from a taxable source. So unless you consider the ISA wholly inappropriate to your circumstances (and this book will help you determine that), then it is likely that it will form an important part of your overall saving strategy.

The structure of this book is important. ISAs have not been conceived in a vacuum, with no effect on the relative attractiveness of other savings media, nor any relative attractiveness based on prevailing tax rates. The ISA will be more appropriate for some age groups than others, and the existence of other investments within one's portfolio, be they endowments, PEPs, TESSAs and so on, will also dictate the relative importance of an ISA to you. So it is vital that having understood what the ISA is, you then learn how to apply it to your own circumstances. No book can cover every individual requirement, so we set out to show you an approach which will work for everybody. It seeks to evaluate the investment strategy you currently have, and explain how and why the ISA should fit in (if at all).

The major point is that you must always start from your own requirements. To begin with the facilities an investment offers, and then to work back to your own circumstances would mean you are having your personal planning dictated by the design of a product. Chapter 3 explains why this is inappropriate.

So you must read the whole book. This is not only because it is likely to enhance your understanding of other investments, but it will save you making the sort of expensive mistakes that can destroy years of investment growth in one fell swoop.

Good luck!!

Chapter One

What Exactly is an Isa?

ISA stands for Individual Savings Account. Launched on the 6th April 1999, it is the Government's current strategy aimed at encouraging saving and hence, what they call, the "supply side" of the economy.

Political Dimension

In order to understand how important this plan may be, you should look at the Government's political motives in introducing it.

On one level it is simply intended to make individuals more prudent with their funds, and discourage spending on consumable items, which has led to many a consumer boom. Such booms mean many imported goods, balance of trade problems, and an economy based on consumption rather than production.

On another level, Governments have been aware of the great demographic problems which are lurking in the future. At present there are two retired people for every individual in full-time employment. By the year 2020 it is estimated that there will be four retired people for each full-time employee. This comes about as a result of people living longer, and retiring earlier. However, there is a major problem in that individuals who have retired may not be able to support themselves. The Government will not be able to afford to do it, nor will the workforce be sufficiently large to be able to support them.

This is where the ISA comes in. Future state benefits will undoubtedly be means tested. Those who have built up a nest egg through the ISA (or any other means), will probably receive less state assistance. It is therefore sensible for the Government to encourage individual saving so that those individuals are less likely to be a burden on the state.

Another political issue is that of making individuals' needs common to those of the country as a whole. Baroness Thatcher began the process by privatising industries and creating the nation of shareholders. By also selling off council houses and helping fuel the domestic housing boom, a whole band of individuals was created whose requirement is for the stability which capitalism generally brings. By making the ISA as simple as possible it may be that even more individuals become "stakeholders" in the country.

Finally, a new broom always sweeps clean, and there is a good deal of this about the ISA.

Who may have an ISA?

The plan will be available to anyone who is a UK resident and aged 18 or over. You are generally considered UK resident if you are here for more than half a year for several years in succession. The majority of adults in the UK should qualify.

How does it work?

The ISA is nothing more than a tax-efficient pot in which you may keep your hard earned savings, be they cash, shares or even life assurance.

Later in the book you will see how the TESSA and PEP used to work, and that the ISA is effectively a combination of the two, albeit with some significant differences.

How much can you contribute?

Each person will have an annual allowance of £5,000. This is increased to £7,000 for the first year only, as a step down from the current £9,000 limits for the old TESSAs and PEPs.

What is inside the ISA?

The ISA can have up to three component parts; Life Assurance, Cash and Shares. Of the £5,000 limit, no more than £1,000 can be placed on-deposit in cash, and no more than £1,000 can be invested in life assurance products. The balance, or the entire amount, can be made up of stocks and shares. (The limits for cash and life assurance were increased to £3,000 for the first year only where the overall limit is £7,000).

Must i split my investment?

You do not have to invest in every component part. You could simply invest £1,000 in cash and leave it at that. You may invest £1,000 in life assurance and leave it at that, or invest only in stocks and shares. You might invest even less than this, but that will depend on product terms. It is, though implicit in the make up of ISAs that there is a need to split investment (forming a mini-portfolio) but this is down to individual preference.

What are Maxi and Mini ISAs?

Some organisations will only offer ISAs which invest in one of the components, such as cash or life assurance. If so, this will be called a Mini ISA. Other organisations will offer ISAs that invest purely in shares, which will be another type of Mini ISA. If there is an investment in all three components, this will be a Maxi ISA.

You can have three different Mini ISAs, choosing a different manager for each component. Which may have an added safety factor, allowing prime expertise to work on your behalf in each area of investment. As with most things, different human beings have different skills so it may be of some use to employ the very best skill for each discipline.

Can I buy the shares of One company?

Under PEP regulations you could buy the shares of one company, in what was known as a single company PEP. This single company investment vehicle has now stopped. However, you may buy shares in individual companies to keep within your Maxi ISA if your provider so allows.

What about my windfall shares?

One of the great attractions of PEPs, was that windfall shares from building society conversions and life assurance company conversions could be sheltered. This will no longer be allowed. Which will be a disappointment to those who have been hanging on to building society accounts in order to gain just such an advantage.

What about life insurance?

This is a significant departure, because PEPs and TESSAs did not allow a life insurance link. However, the ISA will. This will be a reassurance to those looking toward their pension. If a death occurs short of the target date for retirement, the life insurance can go a some way to making up the short fall. Tax concessions on life insurance premiums were withdrawn in the 1984 budget so investment opportunities offered by insurance policies have been considerably reduced since then. ISAs change this.

It is expected that individuals can invest up to £1,000 a year in a life assurance product which will then be tax-free. The type of policy that covers your car or your home against loss or damage doesn't qualify as an investment, but any insurance scheme that pays you something at the end of its term (whether or not the catastrophe against which you are insuring happens) may be worth considering. So far, there has been little from the insurance world on this, who may consider it too small an investment unit to be economic.

If the insurance company fails, insurance is covered in law by the Policy-Holders Protection Act. The Policy-Holders'

Protection Board makes sure that you can recoup 90% of any outstanding return promised under the terms of the agreement, provided the promises were reasonable.

Can I transfer my ISA?

There should be full transferability between ISAs, but for the first year all such transfers will have to be on a like-for-like basis. For example, a cash based Mini ISA will have to be transferred to another cash based Mini ISA. In the longer term though you may be advised to transfer an investment to prevent a catastrophic loss. In this case transferability is essential.

Just imagine if all your investment is with one company and you hear that the company is in financial difficulty and you are going to incur losses. You need to act to minimise those losses. Imagine if you were not able to transfer your investments and all you could do was watch as a company's decline took with it all your hard earned cash - remember Polly Peck and Ferranti!!

What will this cost the Government?

Statistics from the Government suggest that the current cost to the Treasury of both PEPs and TESSAs in the region of £1.5 billion per annum. This is expected to rise to £2.5 billion per annum by the year 2005. Given that the total ISA limit will be less than half the combined PEP and TESSA limits, this suggests the Government is expecting over three times as many account holders for the ISA than there previously were for PEPs and TESSAs. In other words, a much wider market penetration. If this expectation is to be fulfilled it could be seen that there would be added advantages to encourage greater uptake of ISAs compared to its predecessors.

Where can I get an ISA?

There will be a bewildering choice of outlets and of ISAs themselves. It will be essential that you get hold of quality information or take professional advice. Buyer beware is the phrase to remember. The banks and building societies will again be to the fore as with PEPs and TESSAs. Supermarkets, with their high throughput of customers, are also likely to provide plans. You must be sure that you have your own understanding of what your savings policy means to you in order to maintain a check on what you are doing and why. Chapter 12 looks at this in greater depth.

What is a CAT?

CAT is an acronym for 'cost, access and terms', and the Government will be awarding the CAT mark to those ISAs which reach the various criteria in these areas. The idea is that a CAT marked ISA will be available at a reasonable cost, with easy access and on fair terms.

There is also a requirement that all advertising and literature should be expressed in plain English. However, it remains to be seen exactly whose English is going to be plain enough to be understood by all those who need to understand it. This could be a key to the overall success of the Government plan to triple the number of account holders in ISAs as opposed to TESSAs and PEPs.

The Government is very well aware of the sort of scandal that surrounded personal pensions and has dogged other investment products in the past. They have a vested interest in it getting right. This is a political development which will have long term effects upon the nation's balance sheet. These long-term effects, rather like the Poll Tax, are very difficult to live down. Clearly, to introduce a new scheme, which failed miserably and led to compensation claims, would be a disaster. Accordingly, they have decided to introduce this system of CAT marking. This is intended to help those individuals who wish to invest but have no experience of having done so.

But is the CAT mark any use?

If the system really gets off the ground, it may well be the most useful benchmark for any ISA investor. There are already a great many big name providers who may have difficulty in reaching the CAT standards. In fact, it has been suggested that most of the National Savings products which are backed by the Government will not be able to meet the CAT standards in their present form. It is perhaps another essential part of getting a high uptake of ISAs. If there is a simple system, which is easy to understand and can be quickly and easily referred to, it is just possible that more people rather than less will start their own ISAs. If it's easy they will do it in numbers, if it's hard they will not.

So is the ISA
completely tax-free?

Not exactly. In the old days PEPs used to be absolutely tax-free, and so were TESSAs. However, any ISA that invests in the stock market, will face a small tax deduction on dividends. Of course, like pension funds there will be a reclaim, but this will only be at the rate of 20% and will be reduced to 10% in subsequent years. From 6th April 2004 there will be no refund at all. What this means is that dividends will not be tax-free, and over the long-term this is a serious issue. It could be seen as an added complication or even a deterrent in the long term to investment in ISAs. Complications in anything prevent people from trying them out in the first place, fearing that they may then need to seek advice later on, creating additional expense. (See the taxation schedules and appendices.)

Can I 'job' in and out of my ISA?

Not quite. If you invest your full allowance, you will not be able to contribute any further until the next tax-year. This applies if you take it out again. So if you put £5,000 in take £2,000 out and wish to replenish that £2,000, you will not be able to do so. Being able to take out a required amount on a planned occasion is an improvement on other long term investments as the money is usually tied up for the duration of the investment period.

Can I switch within the ISA?

The answer to this question is not simple. The ISA rules say that money contributed to the cash component of a Maxi ISA has to remain in cash and cannot be switched into the investment component. Further, any money invested in the investment component of the Maxi ISA will not be capable of conversion into the cash component. This all applies to a Maxi ISA.

However, you can still move from your investment Mini ISA into a Mini cash ISA and back again (remember that cash held in an investment Mini ISA suffers a flat rate charge of 20% deducted from any interest earned).

The effect of this means that for the first time investors will be able to manage their stock market investment by moving in and out of cash as applicable. This was not previously possible under the PEP regime.

What will happen to My existing PEPs?

There is no need to do anything about your existing PEPs. You can leave them to simply accrue more value (hopefully) with the current fund manager.

What if my fund manager decides not to run PEPs anymore or starts to have poor investment performance?

All is not lost. You can still transfer between PEP managers, and there is likely to be a great deal of activity in this regard. In fact, the end of new funding for PEPs is probably a good time to consider the schemes you have and see whether or not they should be consolidated under one roof.

It is the same with ISAs as with PEPs, you will be looking for low charges consistent performance and the widest possible spread of risk. A tracking fund is one way of achieving this without much thought or effort on the behalf of the purchaser. However, people  with experience in the investment market may be think they can spot the outstanding fund manager. If you are one of these, then you should consider the following questions:

- Has outstanding past achievement been against the index or just against other companies?
- How much of the fund manager's previous record was skill as opposed to luck?
- Can you see a good reason for this achievement continuing in the future?
- Is this good performance achieved year on year?
- Will your fund manager still be there year on year (Only 3.5% of Fund Managers are still with their fund after 10 years)?

But what will happen To my TESSA?

The situation with TESSAs is different. You cannot simply go on holding them outside of the ISA as you can with your existing PEPs. However, you will be allowed to convert an existing TESSA into a cash ISA so that you can continue to get the tax benefits. Thankfully, converting an existing TESSA into an ISA does not count towards your current allowance, so it should be quite possible to hold a considerable amount of cash by converting a TESSA.

Does it matter how old my TESSA is?

Yes it does. If your TESSA matured before the 5th January 1999, then your original TESSA capital may be rolled over just like the present system. This would give you a new TESSA, which would go on for a further five years.

If your TESSA should mature after 5th January but before the end of the 1998/99 tax year, you can either roll over into a follow on TESSA, or convert into a cash ISA.

If your TESSA matures after the start of the 1999/2000 tax year, you have a six-month deadline from the maturity date during which you can convert the TESSA into an ISA in order to retain the tax advantages. It is important to make good use of the six months grace that you have before converting your TESSA into an ISA.

> **In the early days of TESSAs there was a story of two chaps who took redundancy, at the same time, with the same payout. The first invested immediately. The second took a little time to shop around for the best deal that he could find. The difference between the two in the final analysis was that the one who shopped around achieved two and a half times more growth than the one who invested immediately. So make good use of the time you have and shop around.**

But where does that leave me in terms of limits?

Well if you convert a TESSA which has matured at say £12,000, you can roll over your £9,000 original capital into a cash ISA during the 1999/2000 tax year, and yet you will still be able to contribute the maximum (£7,000) to a brand new ISA for that year. You can even include the £3,000 cash ISA component if you want to, so that you will effectively have £12,000 of cash in your ISA.

With the limits now reduced, is it worth having an ISA with a £5,000 maximum?

£5,000 invested every year for the ten years during which the Government has guaranteed the ISA will be available, should mature with a value of almost £80,000, assuming 10% annual rate of return. We all learned the lesson of PEPs which began in a very humble way and went on to provide many six-figure portfolios.

Is an isa the answer to all investment needs?

Not quite. You need to consider the chapters which outline how an ISA fits in as part of an overall financial plan, but the majority of investment needs are capable of being met via an ISA.

Chapter Two

How to Create a Financial Plan

There is little point in reading the press and a few leaflets, and then nipping down to the supermarket to open an ISA. This is not likely to produce the best results for you. It is not that you have to carry out masses of research, because this is often available cheaply or even free through financial advisors, on the Internet, or in consumer magazines. (In each case, you will need to understand the spin which is put on all this information.)

The approach you should take however, is to begin by defining your own needs and then see where the ISA fits in.

Start With You

You must remember that money, and money expressed in the form of investments, is nothing more than a tool to achieve your aims.

You can demystify the whole complicated jungle by simply deciding what you want and holding on to those requirements precisely and tenaciously.

Defining Your Requirements

Perhaps one or two examples will show you how this approach works.

Imagine a married man with two young children. He has a company pension scheme but his wife is not in employment. He finds that after having paid his mortgage and the endowment, which supports it, he has a certain amount of money left over. Immediately he is confronted with choices. Should he pay AVC's to his company pension scheme? Should he increase his endowment? Should he put money in the bank? Is it the best time to change the car? Should he take a chunk out of the mortgage? All of these considerations are likely to cause confusion.

Now imagine the same man were to sit down with his wife and decide exactly what they want. He might end up with a list like this.

1. We want to retire when we are 60.
2. We want a spendable income at that point of £12,000 a year.
3. In the meantime we want to ensure we always have £5,000 in the bank which we can raid when there is some unforeseen expenditure, such as a major car breakdown or the need to repair the house after a storm.
4. We don't like risk in investments.
5. We don't pay high rates of tax.
6. We are very disciplined people who want flexibility because we know that we won't fritter money away.

By looking at these aims, you can immediately see that paying Additional Voluntary Contribution's to a pension (where they would be locked up until 60) might not be the right answer. Putting the money in the stock market would not suit the statement about low risk. Chasing enterprise investment schemes or other "tax-efficient" investments would not suit either, because as lower rate taxpayers this is unlikely to yield much benefit and can be high risk. Little by little, by defining the aims they have and discussing their circumstances they can start to rule out certain investments.

Take another example. Imagine a single man or woman with a mortgage well within their capabilities of payment. They have no pension scheme, no life assurance, but have saved £12,000 in a building society. Their aims might be as follows.

1. To make sure that after their death there are no problems left behind in settling their estate for their parents.
2. To ensure that in the case of illness they would not be reliant on the state.
3. To go on working, even part-time in retirement.
4. To take a risk in investment and enjoy being involved with it's management.

Straight away, it becomes apparent that this person does not need life assurance (because the mortgage will be paid off and there will be spare cash to help with funeral expenses and so on). But he or she certainly does need a Will (In order to ensure there are no complications for those parents left behind). As he or she would like to go on working until well beyond retirement age, then the funding for a pension need not be so critical. What would be critical however, is the need for some sort of insurance cover against illness or injury so that there would not be a dependence on the state. As for the funds in the bank, perhaps some could be introduced into the stock market with the investor choosing one or two shares that they think might do well.

You will see that in both these examples investments start to make much more sense when they are suited to an individual's stated requirements. On their own, investments seem to be nothing more than a way for the sponsors to make profit. But used correctly they can actually open up a whole range of opportunities to meet your requirements.

You may have noticed that we have not yet mentioned an ISA for any of these people. Let's see how it might work for both examples.

The married couple do not like investment risk. Hence, if they do have an ISA they are likely to concentrate on the cash element. The fact that the money will always be accessible should not be an issue, because they have emphasised their financial prudence and discipline. Whilst they are not higher rate taxpayers, they will nonetheless be sheltering from tax within the framework of the plan. If they build up enough money in ISA, at some time in the future they might be able to start reducing their mortgage, or accelerate retirement should their plans change. For this couple then, an ISA is very useful.

For the single person the ISA could also be a benefit. This is because it would be an excellent way into the stock market. The plan holder would get a tax-free return on capital growth and a degree of shelter on dividends, and could tune the investment risk to suit themselves. At times when profits are available, perhaps the mortgage could be reduced. In fact, one could argue that the amount saved in income tax, could then be used to buy the health or injury insurance referred to earlier.

It would be a rare situation where an ISA was not able to work its way into an overall plan, but it would be a poor use of the ISA not to create that plan clearly in the first place and ensure that the ISA fits.

Defining Your Aims

The aims defined in the examples above were of course rather simple and entirely fictitious. When you come to define your aims, you will need to think about it very carefully.

You will need to divide your aims into short, medium and long-term. Otherwise you might run the risk of having an excellent long-term financial plan that prevents you living in the meantime.

Short-term aims could include objectives such as saving for this year's holiday, or perhaps for the deposit for a new car.

Medium term aims can vary with age, in that for someone in their late fifties the 'medium term' could include retirement. Generally, however, medium term would mean between one and five years. This could still include saving for a particularly expensive holiday, such as a trip to Disneyland. Alternatively, having just changed your car you might begin a sort of "sinking fund" for the next one or consider upgrading the model.

Longer-term aims would be for periods exceeding five years. The most classic example of this, would be planning for your retirement, although planning for private and university education for your children or grandchildren also generally falls into this category.

Safety

In the case of stocks and shares compensation can be obtained from a stock exchange fund in the case of fraud or failure by stock exchange members. You cannot, of course, be compensated for losing money by investing in the wrong shares.

Stock market prices depend not only on supply and demand, but also on the judgement of each individual investor's point of view. This means that the merest nuances have an effect, varying from newspaper articles, the state of the economy to the chit chat of those in the know, international affairs, rumours of take-overs, even something as mundane as the weather.

Violent fluctuations in share prices are usually ironed out by the sheer size of the markets. When one share drops in price, due to an individual or institutions opinion, there will be another individual or institution who now considers it a bargain. Similarly, if a share rises rapidly in value, some investors in that stock will want to realise a profit and start selling, thus causing the price to drop.

Even so, over time, individual shares can vary quite considerably in value. Some, such a the blue chips, or largest companies, are considered to be relatively safe, and should not drop too much in overall value. This is because they are well diversified and a drop in one of their markets can be offset by an improvement in another.

Consider, for example a company such as the oil giant BP. If the price of oil goes up, it benefits from it's exploration activities, so it can sell the oil at a higher price. If the oil price drops, however, the downstream side of the business, will benefit by selling a cheaper product to the customer at the petrol pumps.

Smaller companies, on the other hand, are more prone to a change in one market. If it experiences a downturn, it may not have another market to turn to. They are, therefore, considered to be 'less safe'.

Risk

You need to decide how much risk you are willing to take on, in order to achieve your various aims. For example, you may decide that you will save for retirement through a variety of different high-risk vehicles such as individual small company shares, or overseas Unit Trusts. Then again, you may be somebody who wants the safety and security of either cash deposits or with-profit pension funds. Either way, unless you define your risk profile carefully, you will be short of one of the major issues you need to address.

Of course, risk need not be one simple statement that covers everything you do. No one needs to be 'low risk' or 'high risk' across the entire range of their investment. What you should adopt is a process known as risk banding. This means you create what is effectively a risk pyramid with lower risk investments at the bottom and higher risks at the top.

For example, a low risk investor might have 25% of their funds in cash, 25% in with-profit schemes. A further 30% might be in Unit Trusts, spread throughout blue-chip equities.

Finally, there could be a small slightly riskier amount in direct share ownership of privatisation issues. This would be a relatively low risk pyramid, even though it contains items with varying differing risk profiles. (See the Appendix for a table of investments defined as to their usual risk.)

A high-risk investor might have no cash at all and simply a 10% base to the pyramid in with-profit funds. A further 50% could be in Unit Trusts, but including smaller company funds and those invested in overseas markets. The higher level could be in Penny Shares or something where there is a strong possibility of losing the entire stake.

Once again, it is a matter of grading the investments and creating a spread.

Generally speaking, a portfolio is considered to be 'sound' if it has a broad base and a narrow top. In other words, one should aim to invest larger amounts in safe deposits or Government bonds, and smaller amounts in small company shares or emerging markets.

Other Types of Risk

Risk is not entirely market risk, that is to say losses caused by fluctuating values of investments. It can also be inflation risk, where the value of your holdings fall behind inflation. Alternatively, it could be the risk of default by institutions with whom you invest. So keep an eye on all forms of risk.

Timescale

Finally, you will need to decide the timescale over which you will express your aims. Will you be judging over months, years or decades.

You will need to define this clearly and you will see how this works in the example right.

Testing your aims for compatibility

It is no good saying "I would like to double my money every six months without risk". These aims are simply not compatible. You therefore need to continually test your aims as you refine them.

Accordingly, "I would like to educate my children privately, will invest £100 a month for five years, and take a medium amount of risk", is a much better aim for being expressed more clearly.

However, it is still incompatible because the amount needed for private education is unlikely to be achieved based on the amount saved. In that example, either the risk reward ratio, the amount of time over which you are saving, or the amount saved will need to be changed.

So even once you have defined your aims, you will have to study them further to make sure they are realistic.

Chapter Three

The Effects of Taxation

The effects of taxation cannot be ignored when you are planning for your savings. Even though we've established that the returns from an ISA are entirely tax-free, this does not mean that you should ignore tax. This is because it effects the relative competitiveness of the ISA itself. For example, imagine if income and capital gains tax were only 5%. It would be hardly worth bothering with tax-free investments at all, particularly if they brought extra costs or other constraints which were not worth the 5%. Conversely, if income tax were 95%, then such tax shelters as an ISA would be absolutely vital.

As none of us knows what tax rates will be in years to come (and bear in mind that PEPs had a life of some 12 years), then it seems wise to consider taxation now in assessing an ISAs relative attractiveness.

The battle for your cash has already started with banks and building societies putting out press releases. For instance, one high street bank has put out a warning that savers "should not be persuaded into taking out a tax-free ISA which only invests in stocks and shares". It goes on to explain that "ISAs will allow you to put £7,000 of savings out of the taxman's reach in the first year. Of this £3,000 could be held in a straight forward cash savings account."

For most people these cash ISAs would be more suitable than shares, it continues. The head of Product Planning and Risk at this particular company is reported as saying "The tax breaks for every £100 invested in a stocks and shares ISA will be worth only around 25p per year to most savers.

Even this small benefit will end in 2004 when the 10% tax credit paid on dividends from UK shares in the ISA will cease. Yet the tax benefits of the cash ISA for basic rate taxpayers will be around four times as much. For higher rate taxpayers the tax benefits will be twice as much."

Do you understand this advice? Probably not! It is important to remember that over the years, on the whole, share based investments have produced higher returns than cash based ones. You may assume this will continue and so the total value of the shares fund of your ISA will grow more than the cash value, irrespective of the tax breaks.

So, to return to the 'advice' given above, this is rather lop-sided and short-termist if your ISA is there to plan for the long-term, but possibly good advice for the short-term. It also serves to highlight the difficulties you will have in understanding 'advice' you see or are given, unless you have a clear idea of your financial planning objectives. Always remember the hidden agenda of the person or organisation giving you advice, particularly if they do not know your personal circumstances.

There is growing concern that people could inadvertently lose most of their potential tax-free saving through making a hasty decision. One investment giant is at the centre of criticism, as they will only be offering a maxi ISA without a cash savings element.

ISA rules allow up to £3,000 in stocks and shares, £1,000 in cash (£3,000 in the first year) and £1,000 in life insurance, each with a different company. But this investment giant is not offering this option, reportedly, thus depriving smaller savers of the chance to benefit from tax free interest on their cash savings. This could well be because they have chosen to pursue the kind of business which is more apt to their kind of operation.

Tax Driven Investments

One very important piece of advice is this – never enter an investment purely because of reasons of taxation. Of course, taxation is a vital feature, but it is nothing more than that. History is littered with examples, be they business expansion schemes, enterprise zone investments, or off-shore arrangements, where perfectly sensible people came a cropper when they took out investments which they would never otherwise have considered, had it not been for a tax benefit.

What you must do is make sure an investment stands up in its own right, and then treat the tax freedom as a bonus.

The Effect of Tax Freedom

There are three major effects of a freedom or relief from tax. The first of these works at the outset, the second works during the life of the investment, and the third on its final encashment. There are therefore, several different permutations of these features. For example, a pension may have tax-relief up front, but be entirely taxable in payment.

An endowment policy has no tax-relief up front but is entirely tax-free in payment. You need to be something of a clairvoyant to figure out which will be the best strategy for you twenty years from now, and of course the answer will be to hold a variety of different instruments of which the ISA would generally be one.

Up Front Tax-Relief

Some investments are increased immediately by tax-relief. The most obvious are enterprise investment schemes, and pensions.

With a pension you currently invest 77 pence, and the investment fund is immediately worth £1. (What is really happening is the life assurance company is claiming the 23 pence – equivalent to the rate of taxation – from the Government). So you can see that the pension is immediately an extremely tax-efficient investment. If you pay 40% tax, then your £1 investment costs you only 60 pence!

An enterprise investment scheme works by giving you 20% tax-relief, which may be rather less attractive but should nonetheless be considered.

Tax Freedom on Growth

Once you have made the investment, the growth thereon can be taxable. For example, if you buy a second home and make a gain then you are likely to pay capital gains tax when you sell it. However, the old style PEP, used to grow entirely free of capital gains tax. This boosted its return considerably.

Tax Freedom on Encashment

Imagine the poor old endowment policy. No tax-relief on the way in, no real freedom from tax on growth, but thankfully tax-free on maturity. That is to say the final proceeds will always be tax-free whatever their size.

A pension conversely, which has the tax relief on the way in, is only very lightly taxed whilst it grows, but the income it provides is entirely taxable on maturity.

How The ISA Fits In

The ISA then has no tax-relief on the original investment. If you invest £1, and ignore any charges, £1 will be invested. It will not be increased by tax-relief. However, the ISA will grow completely free of all capital gains tax (on its growth), and also free of most income tax, for example on interest.

Finally, the proceeds of an ISA will be entirely tax-free in the hands of the recipient. So how does this stack up against the opposition?

The Effect Of Tax-free Roll-up

Columns 1, 2, 4, 5 and 7 in the table below show no tax relief at the outset and the different effect of gross roll-up and taxation of the proceeds. Columns 3 and 6 show 20% initial tax relief and the different rates of tax on the proceeds. Finally, Column 8 shows the effect of 40% initial tax relief and 20% tax on the proceeds.

	1	2	3	4
Starting Figure	£1,000	£1,000	£1,250	£1,000
Proceeds	£2,590	£2,159	£3,237	£2,590
Net Proceeds	£2,590	£2,159	£2,840	£2,590

	5	6	7	8
Starting Figure	£1,000	£1,250	£1,000	£1,667
Proceeds	£1,791	£3,237	£2,590	£4,234
Net Proceeds	£1,791	£2,442	£2,590	£3,793

Key

1. No tax relief, tax free growth, tax-free proceeds
2. No tax relief, growth taxed at 20%, tax-free proceeds
3. Tax relief at 20%, tax-free growth, proceeds taxed at 20%
4. No tax relief, tax-free growth, tax-free proceeds
5. No tax relief, growth taxed at 40%, tax free proceeds
6. Tax relief at 20%, tax free growth, proceeds taxed at 40%
7. No tax relief, tax free growth, tax-free proceeds
8. Tax relief at 40%, tax-free growth, proceeds taxed at 20%

As you will see from these tables, the relative merits of each investment change when the tax regime changes.

Conclusion

The role of the ISA then is likely to be important for most investors. This chapter should have demonstrated the workings, and the potentially considerable importance of the tax-benefits.

For those people with only a short period over which to save, the lack of up front tax relief is likely to prove a disincentive.

For those with a longer savings horizon, the fact of the investment rolling up almost completely free of tax, and providing entirely tax-free proceeds, is likely to prove decisive.

Chapter Four

Shares

You may already know some of the information contained in this chapter, especially if you have been active in the markets before this point. Even so, it is worth re-visiting this ground as it will help re-focus your activities and keep you within accepted investment 'best practices'.

Stocks and shares are bought and sold through middlemen known as brokers. The world's stock markets work much like any other market except here the commodities are stocks and shares.

Companies issue shares to raise money, and in doing so offer the general public a share in the financial future of the company. They may wish to raise money to fund some type of expansion or simply to avoid taking out a loan. If, for example, the company took out a loan, the interest on that loan would be payable whatever the performance was of the company. If the money is funded by shareholders though, the improvement in performance is passed on to the shareholders. A good per-formance means a good dividend and a rising share value - a poor performance means a lower dividend and a dropping share value. Whatever happens the com-pany has shared its risk with its shareholders.

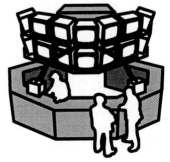

There are a number of types of shares:-

Ordinary Shares, also known as equities, are the most common type of share. These are usually recognised as giving the owner rights at shareholder meetings. The ordinary shareholder is the last to get his money back in the case of the company going bust and it is important to be aware that this can happen. Ordinary shares issued by the largest companies are called Blue Chip shares and are deemed to be as safest form of ordinary shares.

Preference Shares, as the name suggests, give preferential treatment to the owner in the case of the company going bust. However it is sometimes the case that the dividend paid on these shares is fixed. Always check the details.

Convertible Preference Shares are changeable into ordinary shares on particular dates at prearranged rates. This gives the holder the opportunity, under a good financial climate, to benefit from capital gain.

Cumulative Preference Shares are the same as preference shares except any dividends which haven't been paid for any reason can be claimed at a later date.

Redeemable Preference Shares have fixed repayment dates allowing the owner to plan their financial affairs with some accuracy. These shares are the closest form of loan you can make to a company.

Deferred shares are shares that do not qualify for dividend until a predetermined date, but they usually confer normal shareholder rights to the owner. They are often given to employees as an inducement to encourage loyalty.

Price changes

Perhaps the simplest reason for a change in share price is that the company concerned is doing well or it is doing badly in its normal trading. If a company were doing well the shares would be more sought after, therefore, the laws of supply and demand dictate a higher price. Conversely, if the company were to do less well then the price of the shares would drop for the same reason.

The overall national economic climate also affects share prices by changing the general disposition of investors. If there is a 'feel-good' factor in the country, investors will feel bullish and put their money into the markets. Lots of factors can contribute to this feel-good factor; media comment, sets of good company results, takeovers, polls of company directors and, of course, rising share prices (yes, it is a self-fulfilling event). Should the general mood be poor, on the other hand, investors will be gloomy and tend to cease investing new money and may even withdraw their cash by selling shares, thus pushing down prices and adding to the gloom.

The Bull Market is one in which the share prices are on an upward movement. Prices may fall back on individual days but in the main the trend is upward. It is thought that the average Bull market lasts three to five years. Often in the early months of a bull market the so-called pundits are already predicting a downturn in the market.

A Bear market is one in which the share prices are on a downward trend. Although prices may also rise for short periods during this time, the general trend is down. This type of market usually lasts for between nine and fifteen months. Of course the pundits are often found to be saying that the upturn is just round the corner, but investors at this time are reluctant to lose any more money.

The Crash is usually a sharp downturn in the market of ten percent or more. There are trends to a crash but it is usually a newsworthy event in itself because it happens suddenly. A stock market crash may appear disastrous but as long as the investor is taking a long-term view the market usually picks up and recovers quickly. The 1987 crash was recovered in two years and could be looked upon as an adjustment to the previous upward trend.

Do you want to invest in the stock market with all these Bulls and Bears crashing about? I guess it's up to you but if you are not involved you do not have the chance to make any gains. On one hand you can argue that it is too risky and you can lose your money. But you can also argue the other way. If you are sitting on the sidelines while all those around you are making money, then you are effectively losing money. That is to say the value of your savings is go-

ing down relative to everyone else. Therefore, non-participation in a Bull market can be considered as 'risky'. Given that Bull markets generally last for four times the length of Bear markets, you could say that it is four times more risky to be out of the markets than in!

Buying
and Selling

There are a number of other factors to consider when buying and selling shares. An institution like a bank will help with your transaction, as would a traditional stockbroker. There are pros and cons of course. A bank may be convenient because they also handle many of your other financial services, but the drawback is that they can be slower to carry out the transaction, they may charge more and their market knowledge will certainly not be as concentrated as that of a traditional stockbroker. Commission rates are often higher with the bank.

However some stockbrokers will only work with a given Minimum of shares, so it pays to check this out at the beginning of your discussion. A broker can make dealing less expensive, faster and a whole lot easier.

It is unlikely that many banks or investment companies will allow you to trade the shares that you are holding in an ISA. They want to make the decisions on your behalf, in part to maximise their profits, but also to cut down on the administration of the ISA. If every ISA holder was buying and selling shares in their ISA, that's many more transactions to follow than if the manager makes the decision that everyone should have a particular share and buys them in a huge block.

Stockbrokers, on the other hand, have an interest in you actively trading your shares. As with PEPs many stockbrokers will be offering ISAs in which you can buy and sell your own choice of shares. You will, perhaps, pay a fixed annual amount for having the ISA umbrella, and then normal transaction costs as you are trading your shares.

Trading is mostly done by telephone. It is usually not possible to deal in exact prices due to the rapid movements of the stockmarket. You may for instance give your instructions based on your knowledge at 10am to your stockbroker and when your broker tries to carry out that instruction at 10.03am and the prices may have changed. You can, however, give instruction to buy or sell at or around certain prices.

When placing your order and calculating the fees that will be attached to it you will need to know the difference between one type of order and another.

- **Market orders.** A market order will be executed by your broker at the best price available at the time. They will not hold onto the order for any time or seek a specific price.

- **Limit order.** In this form of order you will specify the top price that you are willing to pay in the case of a purchase or the minimum price you will accept if you are selling. If these prices are not achievable then your order will not be executed.

- **Stop order.** When the price reaches that set by a stop order then the order will become active and the transaction will take place. This only guarantees that the transaction will actually be executed and does not fix the price.

- **Stop-limit orders.** This is like the combination of a stop order and a limit order. When a share price reaches a pre-determined price the order is activated. But with a stop-limit order this will be cancelled again if the maximum or minimum prices stated are not available.

- **Day order**. A day order is only valid for the day on which it is placed. If it can not be executed within that date then it will be cancelled.

- **Good-till-cancelled.** This form of order is exactly what it says. It remains in the market and can be executed at any time providing the agreed prices are achieved unless it is cancelled by the person who has placed the order in the first instance.

Pooled Share Funds

Unit Trusts are run by investment companies that allow a group of investors to pool their monies in order to create a varied portfolio of investments and to spread the risk. The investment decisions are then made by the Unit Trust company. Some Unit Trusts encourage investors by enabling investment on a regular basis. It is thus possible to invest as small an amount as £25 per month. Check out the performance of a Unit Trust before getting involved. The past performance of a Unit Trust company does not guarantee

future performance but it should help you feel more comfortable about your investment. The majority of companies offering investment ISAs will be those that run their own Unit Trusts and your share investment will be via the Unit Trust vehicle.

Investment Trusts are companies whose sole purpose is to invest in other companies; they issue shares and are quoted on the stock market themselves. An Investment Trust has more flexibility than a Unit Trust. They will invest money in property, borrow money for investment purposes, buy shares in unquoted companies. Within limits an Investment Trust can generate money whichever way it can, this is because it is a company not just a pool of money like a Unit Trust. Also once all the shares in an Investment Trust are sold no more are generated. This can create price changes with the Investment Trust, as demand goes up and down. If you open your ISA through a stockbroker, it will probably be possible to hold shares in an Investment trust as you would in any other company. This will allow you to take advantage of pooled investing, and to hold individual shares, within the same ISA.

The Role of the Press

While professional advice is necessary you should also keep an eye on what is happening in the press.

In other words the more knowledge you have the greater your chances of success. The best place to find share information is in the financial pages of the daily broadsheet newspapers, and in specialist publications such as *The Financial Times* and the *Wall Street Journal.*

Overall the press is the main source of information (as opposed to share prices) for investors so it is useful to watch the papers to see what other people are likely to do and then you can decide on your course of action. The share prices printed in the press should be viewed as general statistics the investor should not ignore. Shares are listed in groups showing which market they are in, such as Financial, Engineering etc which can help you find them quickly.

Newspapers inevitably print investment tips and, of course, as these are read by a large number of people, they can affect the market place. Knowing what has been tipped as a 'buy' or 'sell' in the financial pages can be considered as crucial information to the speculative investor who makes money out of share movement.

Most publications list the notable 'Director Dealings' in their own company shares. Keep an eye on what they are doing. It makes sense that those people who are directly involved with a company are likely to have more information than the average investor.

Just about all publications will publish the names of companies that are about to produce their year-end or interim results. Beware of rapid share price movements during this period. There are three options. Either the company will announce profits in-line with market expectations and the share price will remain stable. The results will be above expectations and the share price will rise. Or the profits will be lower than estimates and the price will drop correspondingly. It is quite common for interim results to be wide of the mark in either direction, and this can prompt heavy sell-offs or large buys.

Evaluating Shares

The price of a share is not a simple figure plucked out of the air. It depends on the overall market's view of the companies prospects. It therefore helps to understand the differing ways of assessing a share value. These techniques allow the investor to compare shares on a like-for-like basis.

There are three main ways of evaluating a particular share, by calculating the Dividend Yield, the P/E Ratio and the Net Asset Values.

The Dividend Yield calculation will help you calculate the income from a particular share. There are two types of calculation. An historic yield calculation and prospective yield calculation.

To calculate the historic yield, first find the gross historic dividend by adding back the income tax to the net dividend. Then calculate how much this is as a percentage of the share. Dividing the gross dividend by the price per share and multiply by one hundred. This would give a dividend yield percentage.

The prospective yield is a little easier as you may as well go straight for the gross figure. By way of example, if the historic dividend was say 20p per share and the company fore-casts a 40% increase then you can estimate the gross pro-spective dividend to be 28p. This can now be used to find out how much this is as a percentage of the share.

To utilise these figures, in the first instance, simply compare with figures of shares in the same market group. Another method is to balance up your portfolio of shares, i.e. Say you have a portfolio which consists mostly of low dividend shares, it is likely they will be of high capital growth. Knowing this enables you to take a decision to balance this out between good capital growth and good income.

The Price Earnings Ratio (P/E Ratio) is used when directly comparing two companies. It indicates the relationship between share price and profit potential of the company which issues it. The calculation works as follows :-

$$P/E \text{ Ratio} = \frac{\text{Share Price}}{\text{Earned Profit per Share}}$$

i.e. If the Share Price =200p and the profit per share is 20p, then 200 divided by 20 equals 10, which is the P/E Ratio. When comparing companies remember to have the comparison as close as possible. The P/E ratio is mostly used when comparing profits between two companies.

Net Asset Value. These figures are often included in a company's half-year or year-end accounts. Dividing the total assets allocated to shares by the number issued arrives at this figure. For example if a company has £2,000 million for ordinary shares and there are 1,000 million in circulation then the Net Asset Value is £2.

The NAV is an indication, and only an indication, of how much a shareholder is likely to receive in the event of the company going into liquidation. To put it in simple terms, for every ordinary share that is held by the shareholder in the event of the company going bust, the investor could expect to receive £2. This calculation can assist in the decision-making procedure when weighing up the risk of investing in a particular company. Never follow any of these figures without seriously considering their credibility.

Penny Shares

These are recognised as being the most exciting type of share in the market, and have a share price of less than £1. When you hear stories of people who have made (or lost) fortunes on the stock exchange Penny Shares are the most visible way this can happen. It has been known for a company to set up with a share price of say 11p and in a very short time, one, two or three years be worth £30 per

share. This means that if you invest in such shares at the outset and hold them at their peak, say a £1,000 investment would give a return of £272,727 in three years. That is a phenomenal achievement.

Penny Share companies are usually companies often just starting out or whose product has not yet become popular. They just need to win a lucrative contract to catch the eye of the shrewd investor and before you know where you are the performance has been noticed and everybody wants a piece of the action and the share price rockets.

Note, however, that just because a company has a low share price, it doesn't necessarily mean it is a small company. It could be that a £2 billion company has issued four billion shares. In this case each share should be worth about 50p, but the company obviously has a lot of assets and isn't likely to disappear or make spectacular growth overnight.

If you wish to become involved in Penny Shares you would no doubt benefit from reading some of the very good books on the subject.

Building a Share Portfolio

The reason for building a share portfolio is the same reason for building an ISA portfolio. It spreads the risk. Because there are different types of shares, for example some with higher dividend, lower dividend, higher risk and/or lower risk, then it pays to have a secure base to your portfolio. You will probably need a good return with good security at the same time.

The watchword with your portfolio is "**balance**".

A good way to achieve this is to apply what some people call the pyramid principle (as discussed earlier). The pyramid principle applies itself to balancing the risks. The portfolio would be set up with three sections. A wide base made up of very secure low yield investments, a smaller mid level of medium risk and medium reward investments and an even smaller tip of higher risk investments which have the potential for higher gain.

The purpose of this principle is to prevent the investor from investing in too large an amount of high risk investments and thus being in the very vulnerable position of losing a large amount of investment in one fell swoop. Let's face it if our investor were a retired person this scenario would be a disaster.

Looking at these three sections to the pyramid in turn. Low risk would be investments like National savings, Fixed interest stocks with low return but good capital safety. You should not consider moving to medium or high risk until a reliable low risk base is established.

Medium risk investments offer a good deal of security but have a higher potential return. Investing in solid and reliable companies that are unlikely to go bust.

The high-risk element should only be put together when the other two elements are in place. This part of the portfolio includes high potential parts like Penny Shares. (High-risk little-known companies with potential which could, of course, go either way.) A good way to look at the split of the pyramid is 50 percent low risk 40 per cent medium risk and 10 per cent high risk or something of that order.

Within this pyramid of investment the ISA comes into its own, fitting very tidily into the mid section of the pyramid,

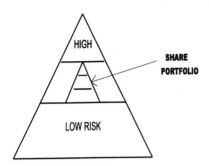

sitting quite comfortably with its own Low, Medium and Higher risk elements. Low being the Insurance part, Medium being the Cash part and High being the Shares part.

When putting a portfolio together it should be done with a specific aim in mind. For instance, someone who is investing for the longer term could actually have three different views on how to go about that investment.

The first may be an all low-risk portfolio and therefore may contain fixed interest stocks as well as high grade blue-chip shares to boost possible gains. The second may be a medium risk portfolio that could contain a variety of blue chip shares that will generate moderate returns and be more likely to survive than, say, Penny Shares. The third would be a higher risk portfolio that would take in a few small cap shares with the possibility of high profits balanced with blue chip shares for stability.

There are several ways of keeping a check on your stocks and shares, usually by charting performance in some form or other. While this form of analysis is used the world over it must be remembered that not one of the calculations that can be used is totally foolproof. They cannot take into account Government announcements or other human reactions to world forces, all of which affect the market place. Most importantly there is no way of predicting a boom or bust situation.

Chapter Five

Bonds and Gilts

Bonds and Gilts can also make up part of your investment portfolio. In the case of stocks and shares an investor is effectively buying a piece of the company, but this is not the same situation with Bonds and Gilts.

- **Bonds** are monies lent to a company and are considered a loan to the company for a given period at a set rate of interest, after which the monies will be repaid.

- **Gilts** are monies lent to the British Government to be used for public works (roads, schools, etc). In return for this money - and this is where Bonds and Gilts differ from stocks and shares - the investor receives a fixed rate of interest as compared with stocks and shares where the investor would receive a variable rate of return called a dividend.

There are several plus points with Bonds and Gilts. They are normally less risky than stocks and shares. If national interest rates fall then the value of Gilts will tend to rise. Purchasing Gilts and Bonds is a relatively simple process and they just about always give a better rate of return than a high street bank deposit account.

It is helpful to remember that Bonds and Gilts are medium risk, medium reward investments.

However, as with all things, there are also several minus points. If the company or Government cannot meet its obligations to the investment, it may default meaning that the investor may get a reduced amount or even none of their investment back at the end of the agreed term. This scenario is, one hopes, highly unlikely in the case of Gilts!

You can also lose out in a raging bull market. When the investment market changes substantially you may find yourself stuck with an investment that is not able to take advantage of those changes. Bonds and Gilts do not have the huge gain potential that stocks and shares have.

> Gilts were originally written
> on gilt-edged paper, hence the name.

A Gilt is the promise by the British Government to repay the money invested on a certain date and to pay interest on the money at a fixed rate during the term of loan. Gilts are exempt from capital gains tax except to the very large investor. Since a Gilt is a deal with the Government it makes them inherently safer than bonds. As with most Bonds, Gilts can be traded at any time, and their prices will rise or fall according to general interest rates at any given time. As a general guide, Gilts are a useful investment in a time of low interest rates.

A Bond is the promise in the same way as a Gilt, except it is a transaction with a company instead of the Government. Bonds take many different forms but all can be long, medium, or short term. "Shorts" as they are known, mature in up to five years. "Mediums" mature between five and ten years. "Longs" mature in more than fifteen years.

Bonds will give you a fixed return, an ease of investment that doesn't tie your money up for long periods and a priority over shareholders in the event of the company going bankrupt. Trading expenses are low compared to other types of investment. There are lots of different types of Bonds from Junk Bonds to Corporate Bonds, Convertible Bonds, Euro Bonds and Zero Bonds to Guaranteed Income Bonds.

Convertible Bond

A Convertible Bond gives the right to convert the bond into a share if required. The Convertible is not liable to Capital Gains tax only if it meets the requirements for and is included in a PEP or an ISA.

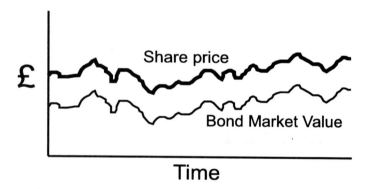

Corporate Bond

A Corporate Bond is exempt from capital gains tax unless you are a very large investor. A Corporate Bond can be either "secured" or "unsecured". With a secured Bond the company will have assets put aside to cover the Bond, but with an unsecured Bond this will not be the case. A secured Bond is therefore quite a safe investment where as an unsecured Bond is not.

Euro-Bond

A Euro-Bond is a bond which will raise money for a foreign company outside its own country. Investment here would involve foreign currency fluctuations as well as fluctuations in the market place. This makes dealing in these kinds of shares very hard to predict.

Guaranteed Income Bonds

Guaranteed Income Bonds are bonds with a set interest rate but which cannot be sold during the life span of the bond. This means that if interest rates drop the investor benefits from a higher rate than is currently available, but if interest rates rise then the investor can be stuck with this investment until it has matured.

Junk Bonds

Junk Bonds are a very risky deal to get involved in because they are shares issued on behalf of a company that has already gone bust. There are large risks with these because it takes a great deal of knowledge to work out if there will be a return on these shares. The return would come from the assets of the company being worth more than is repayable to the secured bond holders.

Zero Bonds

Zero Bonds are bonds sold at a greatly discounted price. The value of a Zero Bond increases until it reaches its redemption value at which point the investor takes his profit on a given maturity date.

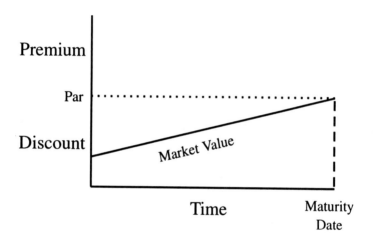

Chapter Six

Pound Cost Averaging

Whilst this book has tried to keep matters clear, and keep jargon to a Minimum, you cannot consider the investment based ISA over the medium or longer-term without an understanding of the phenomenon known as Pound Cost Averaging.

Imagine you are investing solely in the UK stock market index whilst it stands at 6,000 points. If you are investing £60 a month, then the amount of index units you buy should be fairly clear. Of course, you would like the index to reach 12,000 points so that you have effectively doubled your money. But when do you want it to do that? The answer to this question is rather complicated.

What you actually want is for the index to stay at 6,000 points for the whole of your savings period, even if it is 10 years. Then you want it to suddenly catch up in the weeks before your plan comes to an end, perhaps rising to 12,000 or 24,000 points to make up for 10 years lost growth. If this happens, then all the units you bought at 6,000 points, from the first month right through to the last months of the tenth year, will suddenly rocket in value.

Conversely, if the market were to rise on a steady incremental basis from 6,000 points to 24,000 points over ten years, then you simply would not make as much money. This is because as time goes by you will buy units at 6,000, 6,100, 6,200 and so on. The units you bought in the tenth year would only increase by a fraction and your overall return for this investment would be £10,800, compared to £14,400 in the first example.

What would be even better, is if the stock market were to fall 6,000 points to 3,000 points and stayed there until the tenth year when it rocketed back 24,000 points. In that case you would acquire twice as many units as in our first example and your return would therefore be £57,600!

Of course, in reality the stock market will generally trend upwards but with a degree of volatility. That volatility will work to your advantage because whenever the index falls below a 6,000 points in our example, you will be buying units at a lower price, and so the average price which you purchase over your savings plan, will be reduced. What few pound-cost-averaging investors understand, is that a steady rise in the index is actually very bad news!

The phenomenon whereby you can end up better off with falling or volatile markets is known as Pound Cost Averaging and will be an important feature of regularly funded investment ISAs.

Cost Averaging really comes into its own when it is used in the real-world environment of a fluctuating market. Consider this ten month scenario:

Month	Invest	Price	Shares
01	£2,000	£20	100
02	£2,000	£18	111
03	£2,000	£16	125
04	£2,000	£18	111
05	£2,000	£16	125
06	£2,000	£18	111
07	£2,000	£20	100
08	£2,000	£22	90
08	£2,000	£24	83
10	£2,000	£26	76

In this scenario you have invested a total of £20,000. Over the ten month period you have accumulated 1,032 shares. Each share is now worth £26, so your £20,000 investment is now worth £26,832. If you have invested all £20,000 at the outset, you would have purchased 1,000 shares, and these would now be worth £26,000. Cost Averaging has therefore helped you to generate an additional £832 over the ten month period.

This might not sound like a great deal to shout about, but when you consider that an the examples provided here are deliberately modest, and that cost averaging is said to work even better in volatile markets, you should be able to conclude that this strategy is well worth investigating further.

Chapter Seven

Risk Profiling

No investment makes sense in isolation. The whole purpose of the approach outlined in this book has been to ensure that you have a co-ordinated strategy which is intended to achieve your aims. The area where most people find dissatisfaction in their investments, is that of risk. So many people bemoan their investments' unsuitability once they have bought it, because they did not ensure that it suited them in the first place. The one issue which causes the most distress, is not taxation, product design, financial strength of the product provider, but it is risk.

This section therefore sets out the risk profile of a wide variety of investments. By using this template you should be able to put together a balanced portfolio, decide what sort of ISA you want and what component part it will represent.

Risk and the ISA

What is likely to make matters more complicated for the ISA investor, is the fact that an ISA can have several different risk profiles. The old style PEP was generally equity based and with the exception of one or two sophisticated guaranteed schemes, would move up and down with the market. The TESSA was always cash based and so would plod along producing a reasonable tax-free cash return.

Accordingly, once you had identified whether you wanted a PEP or a TESSA, risk was not such an issue, that decision having been already made by selecting the PEP or TESSA in the first place. With the ISA of course, matters are not so simple. You will probably have concluded that you should have one, but whether you have a cash based ISA, an equity based ISA or some sort of mixed ISA would depend on your purpose.

The table below sets out the varying different degrees of risk attaching to a variety of investments. As you will see, the ISA appears in every category and you should be able to decide which ISA to have, based on tracing through this table. Of course, if you are taking advice then your advisor should be able to give you some clear indication as to the degree of risk involved.

(Several ISA providers are aware that there could be problems with investors buying the wrong account, or the right account with the wrong risk profile. They have therefore started a very simple risk rating table with crosses, ticks, exclamation marks and so on. It would be extremely useful if the entire investment world were to adopt this simple but effective statement of risk.)

Finally, do not forget about risk banding detailed in the text. (This is the process whereby you build up a series of differing risk bands, which overall form part of your risk strategy.)

What is your risk profile?

LOW	-	use the green chart
MEDIUM	-	use the amber chart
HIGH	-	use the red chart

The Green Chart

Tax Rate		
NIL ▼	**24%** ▼	**40%** ▼
Consider ▼	Consider ▼	Consider ▼
Cash*	ISA*	ISA*
Gilts	Gilts	Low yielding Gilts
With Profit Policies	NSCs	NSCs
	With Profit policies	Guaranteed Bonds
	Guaranteed Bonds	Guaranteed ISA
		With Profit policies

Indicates regular saving available

The Amber Chart

	Tax Rate	
NIL ▼	**24%** ▼	**40%** ▼
Consider ▼	**Consider** ▼	**Consider** ▼
Cash*	ISA*	ISA*
Gilts	ISA*	ISA*
Corporate Bonds	Gilts	NSCs
Non-specialist Unit Trusts	Unit-linked policies*	Unit-linked policies*
Guaranteed equity funds/ Trackers	Non-specialist Unit Trusts*	Non-specialist Unit Trusts*
CAUTION !	Guaranteed equity funds/ Trackers	Guaranteed equity funds/ Trackers

* Indicates regular saving available

The Red Chart

Tax Rate		
NIL ▼	**24%** ▼	**40%** ▼
Consider ▼	Consider ▼	Consider ▼
Cash*	ISA*	ISA*
ISA	EIS	VCTs/EIS
Individual equities	Individual equities	Individual equities
Specialist* unit and Investment Trusts	Specialist* unit and Investment Trusts	Specialist* fund insurance Bonds
		Woodlands options

* Indicates regular saving available

Chapter Eight

Investment Efficiency

The ISA needs to provide some sort of investment efficiency otherwise it will die out very quickly. What we mean by this, is that if the ISA does nothing for you which you could have done yourself without its existence, then you will soon realise that it is of no added value.

If you take a pension as an example, then in the first instance it obtains tax relief, which is very useful indeed. Secondly, it allows you access to investment markets all over the world with your £50 a month, which would not otherwise be the case. Finally, you are entitled to a degree of protection from bad advice or default on the part of the pension scheme. All of these are valuable features.

Everybody is clear on the potential tax efficiency of an ISA. Chapter Three shows the effect of reduced tax on an investment in pounds and pence. However, in addition to tax efficiency there must be investment efficiency.

What we mean by this is that the investment itself must offer some sort of benefit not otherwise available to the investor. If an investor could replicate the scheme himself, then there will be no need for that scheme.

So What Are The Efficiencies?

Individual investors would find it extremely difficult to put together an ISA on a DIY basis. To find a life assurance company willing to take a certain amount, and a cash deposit provider, along with a stock market link, would be well nigh impossible at the sort of levels we are talking about.

Further, it is extremely difficult and not at all cost effective to invest small amounts in the stock market. If dealing commission is £20, and you have to pay this on purchase and sale of shares, and there is a difference in the buying and selling price, then deals of any less than £1,000 or so become very inefficient. Where the ISA will score, is by allowing individuals to invest relatively limited amounts on a fairly random basis at a very low effective percentage cost.

Indeed, one of the major attractions of the PEP in its hey day was that investors could fund the scheme monthly, from as little as £25 a month. Effectively, the investor was buying in to expert fund management spread throughout nearly all world stock markets. His £25 was being dealt with in the same way as someone else's £25,000 might be dealt with. Without such access to pooled funds, the ISA investor would have to accumulate cash for years until there was a sum big enough to invest in stock. Moreover, if an individual wanted active investment management, then the sum might need to be a six-figure amount before it could be managed effectively! So the economy of scale provided by pooled funds is a crucial feature of the ISA.

Cash Rates

Similarly, cash rates have always been tiered. This means that the investor with £1 could never get the interest rate available to the investor with thousands. However, partly as a result of the electronic age, it is expected that rates of interest for smaller investors will be higher than usual, because the ISA provider will be grouping all funds together and dealing with them on a fairly automatic basis.

Costs of Investing

Of course, one of the issues which is of great importance to busy people, is the amount of time they expend in arranging investments.

I know of many professional people or business owners who are so busy earning a living, that to stop doing so means an immediate loss of turnover. If you are a doctor charging £150 an hour for consultations, then if you spend two or three hours with an advisor and a further two or three hours thinking through an investment, followed by some form filling and checking the documents when they arrive, you have effectively spent £1,500. Can you imagine the effect that would have on a £5,000 ISA!

Accordingly, for the first time investments of this nature are going to be available at supermarkets. So instead of having to go somewhere particular, or meet somebody at their office or yours, you should be able to make deposits very simply while shopping. This should help make the ISA far more useful for many people.

Chapter Nine

Uses of an ISA

So now you know what an ISA is, the basics of how it works, and why the Government has introduced it, the next most important topic to address is how the ISA can be used.

You will see that the aim of this book is not only to give you the important information about the ISA, but to help you understand that it is only one component of an overall financial plan. The uses to which you put the scheme, will depend on your plan, and your aims, which previous chapters helped you to define.

Short and Long-term Savings

Whilst it may appear to be an arbitrary distinction, it is important to differentiate between your short-term savings, and your long-term savings, even splitting down into a third category of medium-term savings if possible. This is because it is important to choose the right type of investment for a particular purpose. For example, imagine you are intending to have a garage built in six months time and have already saved up the money. To put it into the stock market might mean it doubles in that six-month period, or it might mean that it halves. Obviously, such an unpredictable and potentially volatile investment would not be suitable. Conversely, if you are planning for a need some

10 years ahead, for example your daughter's wedding, then it would be foolish to invest in an ISA with too low a risk/reward ratio, when you might benefit more in the long-term capital increases of the stock market.

As for the categories themselves, there is clearly some overlap, and categories can mean different things to different people. For example, if you are in your late fifties then short-term can mean retirement! The next few sections deal with simple uses of the ISA beginning with the shorter-term requirements and moving on to the longer-term.

Very Short-term Requirements

Let us imagine you need money within a year. This might be for a holiday, to decorate your home, or to build up the deposit for a new car. In this case you can really only consider cash as the underlying investment, but why should you chose an ISA?

If you are to save up in cash, then you might as well save up on a tax-free basis. Even if you end up taking out the money within a few months, then  you will at least be ahead by the amount of tax you have saved. This is very significant. In the past, the TESSA would have made sense for short-term investors, were it not for the fact that it has a five-year invest-ment period! So anybody needing money in the short-term could not use a TESSA. Those who did had to wait five years, and so one wondered about the wisdom of the TESSAs' existence at all, given the excellent returns normally achieved by real assets over a five-year period. Such real assets were excluded from the TESSA! So this really is new ground – the ISA is available and suitable for very short-term savings needs.

Incidentally, there are so many people who start to save for a short-term purpose and then find they do not need the funds they have saved for that purpose. Hence, what starts off as a short-term saving becomes a long-term matter. To have left it in the bank on a taxed basis would therefore turn out to be a very poor result in retrospect. With the new ISA you will be able to start off in cash, and if you find you do not need the money and can take a longer-term view you will be able to switch into the stock market, or the insurance component.

Less Short-term Needs

Of course, we all have needs that are annual and recurring, maybe in the period up to say 24 months. Perhaps one might be saving for a holiday, or starting some sort of sinking fund to replace a car which might be between say 12 and 24 months from the time when you start saving. Similarly, some expenditure on the family home, such as exterior decoration or replacement carpets can often be more than 12 months away.

Once again, the cash ISA would be suited to this. Over a good two-year period the compounding effect of the interest and the tax freedom, would start to come into its own. Once again, it would not be appropriate to have an investment based ISA where the fluctuations in value could catch you out. Imagine there were a stock market crash just before you need the money for your holiday or new car. You would then find yourself in a worse position than if you hadn't bothered with an ISA at all.

Medium-term Aims

Once again, this definition will be fairly personal, but I think it is clear that anything which falls in the area beyond 24 months, and perhaps shorter than seven years would be considered medium-term.

Such aims might include saving for your children's weddings, or for a bit of assistance once they go to University. I know many people who tend to save for landmark events like their 50th birthday or 25th wedding anniversary. Of course, depending on the ages of your children, you might also be saving for school fees. Unless you are talking about the holiday of a lifetime or a very unusual car purchase, this type of aim generally falls within the 0-3 year category.

The difficulty with applying the ISA to these requirements is that there is a good argument for staying in cash for the shorter periods but being invested in the stock market for the longer periods. But there is a further complication. You need to assess the purpose for which you are saving, and see whether or not it would be disastrous to undershoot the requirements. For example, imagine your budget for the holiday of a lifetime is £10,000, you should ask yourself how much damage it would do to that holiday if you only made £9,000? You could probably trim one or two elements of the holiday in order to make the savings fit. But if you were saving for the known requirement of school fees, it is unlikely that the school in question would allow you to excuse your child a few lessons in order to reduce the fee!

Accordingly, for this type of saving you need to start considering risk in greater detail. Once again, although the medium-term aims which are reasonably close (before five years), then if you need safety you should be in cash. If alternatively, a shortfall would not be a problem, then you can take the risk of the stock market. For those medium-term aims which are further out in time, then the stock market should be the answer, unless of course the risk of shortfall is too much to bear.

Longer-term Aims

Once you have settled on a term of at least five years and probably longer, then the choice of ISA becomes much

simpler. Those people funding for the very long-term, such as with an ISA mortgage, or those people planning for a supplementary retirement income, usually take a long-term view. If this is the case then the superior return available from the UK stock market judged over five-year periods, will generally mean a much higher rate of return. It is very significant that even a bad PEP generally outperformed the best TESSA. Whilst the best PEPs produce a return so far in excess of the best TESSA, that there really is no quibble about the superiority of equity returns over the long-term. Hence, for long-term education needs, retirement or the repayment of a mortgage, a share based ISA will usually be the answer.

The With-profit Endowment

These schemes function by investing your money in a broad spread of assets within a life assurance company's with-profit fund. However, your fortunes are not directly linked to the fluctuations in those asset values in the first instance, although over the long-term they will be. What happens is that each year the bonus rate is declared on your savings. On a true with-profit endowment, once you have been credited with that bonus rate, it cannot be removed. As time goes by you may be given further interim bonuses until your plan matures, at which point you will receive a terminal bonus.

This approach has the benefit of providing a steady and reasonably predictable return, which is not far off that provided by managed stock market funds, but without the volatility.

Accordingly, the people who require something relatively low-risk, but which combines some of the certainty of cash, with much of the higher growth available from stock market investment, the with-profit endowment will still be important.

Further advantages are the fact that it provides a certain amount of life assurance cover, and that the proceeds are entirely tax-free. Additionally, it can be written in trust which can help with more complicated tax planning issues. Of course, compared to an ISA you may find that the costs are higher, and you will certainly find that the lack of flexibility is a problem. Certainly nobody with short-term savings needs should consider a with-profit endowment, and only those with the longer end of medium-term aims, or long-term aims should really become involved.

Conclusion

You will see that the ISA is therefore a very useful investment tool that can be adapted to suit almost any investment purpose. We have yet to see whether or not the extreme flexibility will actually turn out to be a hindrance, but for those serious-minded and disciplined investors, the ISA should be capable of meeting all their needs in whole or in part.

This may seem like a large claim, but it is quite feasible that the ISA will be capable of replacing the TESSA, the PEP, the unit linked endowment, the National Savings regular savings plans, ordinary regular savings plans with banks and building societies, and even Friendly Society tax exempt plans. The one scheme which the ISA will not be able to compete with is the with-profit endowment.

Chapter 10

ISA/PEP Mortgages

One of the major concerns of investors with PEP mortgages is how these will be dealt with under the new rules. After all, with PEPs coming to an end there is some concern that holders will be left with no means of repaying their mortgage. This section is intended to deal with those problems.

How a PEP mortgage works

In most mortgages, there is a need to repay interest during the term of the loan. This is generally paid monthly. With a repayment mortgage there is also a small amount of capital paid so that the loan diminishes over time. However, with an interest only loan, the amount of capital borrowed at the outset remains outstanding throughout the term of the loan. This means there needs to be some method of repaying that capital at the end of the loan.

An example

Imagine somebody borrows £50,000 from the building society at an interest rate of 8%. Broadly speaking they will need to pay some £4,000 of annual interest, probably paid monthly. However, at the end of the loan (say 25 years later), they will still owe £50,000. The value of the property may well have risen, but it would be foolish to be forced to sell it in order to repay the original loan. Accordingly, there needs to be some sort of "repayment vehicle". For years the only real choice was the with-profit or unit linked endowment. However, for a variety of reasons it became more appropriate for many investors to save through a PEP.

Hence, in addition to the amount of interest paid each month to the lender, the borrower would fund a personal equity plan on a monthly basis, in the belief that it would grow over time to the point where it would be worth £50,000 after 25 years. Thus, the loan could be repaid with a final payment, and the individual would own the house outright.

The problem

There are now a great many people who are well into their PEP mortgages. They may have been funding them for years. Accordingly, they will need a new repayment vehicle once they are no longer allowed to fund their PEPs.

Thankfully, the ISA can do this.

In fact, many PEP providers are simply sending out documentation whereby the PEP can be stopped and the new ISA begun in an almost seamless transfer.

The Pitfalls

PEPs offered very limited opportunities for holding cash. Broadly speaking they would be equity based and the general trend of share prices increasing more rapidly than inflation or interest rates, would mean that a real return would be achieved and the target for redeeming the mortgage also achieved.

One problem from which ISAs may suffer, is that they can be wholly or partly invested in cash. Of course, cash is very unlikely to increase in value at a rate sufficient to repay a future mortgage. This leaves mortgage providers with a problem.

If they were to insist that the individual buy a share based ISA, then they would possibly be liable in the event that the share based ISA did not reach its target for redeeming the mortgage. Alternatively, if they leave individuals to make their own choices, then they might choose a cash based ISA with disastrous results. This problem has barely been addressed by the investment community and as yet there are few practical and acceptable solutions.

What to do next?

Those people who have a PEP mortgage should review the value of their funds and ask the lender to give them a new projection as to the amount of funding necessary to meet the target figure.

Depending on the PEP manager, it should be possible to re-direct regular funding straight into an ISA which holds very similar or even identical underlying funds. In that case, there should not be an issue, unless the mortgage were sufficiently large to require a supporting PEP funded at the previous maximum level of say £9,000 a year. In that case, with a future ISA limit of only £5,000 a year, such PEP holders will be forced to use an alternative method of funding to supplement the ISA. This could see a new re-birth of popularity for the with-profit endowment.

Chapter Eleven

How to Get an ISA

This section is intended to give guidance on how all investors, be they first time plan holders or more sophisticated investors, can go about obtaining a competitive ISA, along with the service necessary to keep the scheme under review. It should help steer you through the marketing minefield, and cut out the ill conceived, and the ill motivated. But remember, caveat emptor applies – this basically means that you have to keep your wits about you, because if you make a mistake then you are likely to suffer the consequences yourself, despite the existence of all sorts of compensation schemes.

Who Will Be The Providers?

You can expect the greatest push on ISAs to be from those people who have been pre-eminent in the PEP market. As far as they are concerned, they will be trying to continue where they left off, retaining all their existing PEP holders as an excellent marketing base, and trying to attract new savers. Hence, the major investment groups such as Perpetual, Fidelity, M&G and so on, will undoubtedly be big players.

The banks will also be looking to exploit their large captive customer bases through cross selling.

Supermarkets will be seeking to use their pre-eminent position in terms of customer traffic and its regularity, to provide plans.

Life assurance companies are likely to be in on the act, because they simply always are, also have a captive customer base, and they're well geared up for marketing drives. Finally, affinity groups such as motoring organisations or other such institutions, are also likely to brand their own ISA.

So where do you start? Can an organisation with an excellent reputation for recovering a broken down motor vehicle, actually make that count in investment? What about the bank that is forever pressuring you to buy something, can they be the right people? Finally, what about the insurance industry, rocked by scandal after scandal in recent years. Can they really be offering an honest product?

The Two Keys

There are two criteria by which you must judge any ISA. These are performance and costs. If the performance of the

investment itself is poor, then however low the costs, it is unlikely to compensate. Conversely, if the investment really does have an edge, then this could be gobbled up by an unfriendly cost structure. One without the other may not be attractive, but if you can combine the two then you surely will produce one of the better ISA returns.

Judging Costs

As soon as all details of the various ISAs were published, research organisations immediately began to consider the costs. These have to be expressed in Government approved format so there is a degree of regularity. It should be possible for any would be investor to obtain details of the costs he or she is likely to pay on a particular scheme.

The sort of cost to which you will need to pay attention include initial costs (for establishing the plan), management costs (for running the plan), and any exit penalties in the event you wish to terminate the plan or transfer it elsewhere.

Discovering the cost structure for you therefore, needs a degree of understanding of your own aims. Imagine for example, a plan were to charge a 3% establishment fee. If you put £1 in it, then you have only paid 3 pence. If you put £5,000 in it, you have paid £150. Conversely, if a scheme charged an establishment fee of £99, then the investor with the larger sum of money, say £5,000, would be paying only 2%, but the investor with £100 will be paying 99%. So you will need to decide what format of charges suits you, based on your likely use for the plan.

This also applies to annual management charges. If there is a set monetary amount, then you will need to see whether or not this is higher than a rival's percentage charge which might be based on the amount you will deposit (or indeed build up over the years).

Additionally, if there are to be exit penalties you will need to see which plan offers the least severe penalty, particularly if you expect to make withdrawals or terminate the plan when you use the funds to meet specific requirements. Some unscrupulous organisations might use the exit penalty as a disincentive for you to leave if their performance is poor.

Finally, there is the hidden charge of lower interest rates. For years building society investors used to claim that where a life assurance company or stockbroker would levy a charge, the building society lets you open up an account without any such charge. How could building societies run national organisations with an outlet in every high street, without incurring some sort of cost? Where could all the money come from?

Well of course, they pay out an interest rate far below that which they actually make from their activities. This is something you will have to watch very closely on the ISA. One organisation may have an apparently high interest rate, but it may only apply to the highest amounts, and there may be hefty monetary charges on the way

in or the way out. Alternatively, other organisations may offer higher rates on smaller amounts, or lower rates with no penalties at all.

Judging Performance

It will be very difficult at the outset to judge the likely performance of an ISA. However, investors will need to make some sort of judgement before proceeding. In the case of PEPs, and this may follow for ISAs also, some investors are not getting the service they deserve from the advisors through whom they made their investment.

Although there is plenty of information around when you are selecting your own personal investment program you are very much left on your own once you have bought it. But the firm that sold you your ISA will receive a payment each year from your fund manager whether or not they continue to provide advice. This renewal commission is typically 0.5% a year of the total value of your Fund.

On a £5,000 general PEP/ISA for instance this amounts to £25 in the first year. As the value of the ISA goes up so does the commission. There is now a battle for this valuable commission and to provide you with a service.

Some companies have already launched an Individual Savings Account and a PEP review service. Investors who switch to these services will automatically receive a valuation of their plans, with figures showing how their funds have performed against competitors and a risk rating on the fund.

The only justification for paying renewal commission is if the agent provides an ongoing service. Some PEP holders currently receive a quarterly bulletin, which contains a monitoring service of all the funds it has recommended in the past along with its current recommendations. One can also receive a recent performance commentary from selected companies, along with a quarterly consolidated valuation of all their plans giving a breakdown of the all markets in which their portfolio is invested.

Others will supply a monthly 'red alert' service, which pinpoints funds whose performance is starting to fall or provide a six monthly valuation

Share Based ISAs

It is not so long ago that there was great kudos in holding shares, even the shares of just one company. This is because it was rare for the average man in the street to be able to afford to own shares at all let alone shares from a portfolio of companies.

> Remember the story of a woman who worked for Walt Disney and was worth millions, but the fact was only discovered on her death. The family found a handful of certificates in a bottom drawer which turned out to be worth a fortune.
>
> The poor lady, who had been a cleaner, had received a certificate every Christmas from the man himself. She thought they were pretty bits of paper and did not understand their true value!

In the UK, the Conservative Government of the eighties and early nineties introduced many ordinary people to the benefits of share ownership. Through the privatisation of many publicly owned industries and allowing the conversion of building societies into banks, many ordinary people have become shareholders in a number of companies. But do they have any idea how their share holdings are likely to perform in the future?

Those people who are looking to invest in the stock market through pooled funds (usually Unit Trusts) have the easiest chance of forecasting the performance of their ISA. They will be able to look at historic performance tables for the major investment groups, and conclude that certain organisations are rather better at managing money than others.

It is the law that investors are reminded that past performance is no guarantee of the future, but in simple terms, it will make more sense to back a proven long term winner than either a new entrant, or an organisation with a history of under-performance.

Whilst on the subject of share based ISAs, there will of course be the prospect of switching between shares and cash. So you will need to see which organisations also offer a reasonable rate of return on dormant cash. Unless you do, whenever you are out of the market, accumulating funds or waiting for a buying opportunity, you may be disadvantaged.

Tracker ISAs

Of course, you need not be concerned about choosing the best fund manager at all. If your requirements are relatively simple, then you could track an index. What this means, is to simply buy into an ISA that takes your money and replicates say, the FTSE Index, or the All Share Index. By so doing, you will broadly receive the performance of the stock market itself, and need not worry too much about your fund manager getting it completely wrong. Whilst you will rob yourself up the prospect of over-performance, you will not be so worried about under-performance, which is actually rather more likely.

Tracker ISAs are likely to be extremely popular because of their simplicity. Organisations should be able to run them relatively cheaply and this aspect of ISAs alone may create a whole new generation of shareholders in the UK.

Cash Performance

Judging cash performance will be extremely difficult. Historic interest rates probably mean very little, whilst forecasting the future is impossible. There are, naturally, banks and building societies with a history (on their ordinary accounts or during the TESSA years), of advertising a high headline rate to get investors in through the door. Once they have the money, they slowly but-surely let rates fall and begin "ISA No 2" with excellent rates to attract another group of new investors. Only the sharpest of investors realise that the excellent rates being offered by their ISA sponsor do not apply to them.

However, there is likely to be a great deal of transferability between providers, so a reasonably competitive interest rate should be provided by most organisations.

By shopping carefully, you can be the beneficiary of somebody's marketing budget. For example, when supermarkets first went into banking, they offered the most attractive rates for very small amounts. They offered rates on £1, that had previously only been available on six figures. Clearly this was a loss leader and an attempt to establish themselves in the market. If you can identify those organisations likely to take this approach, you can win the ISA game (see Appendix II).

It may be possible that if the Government's targets for ISAs are not reached, then further inducements will be contrived to 'up the interest' in this form of public saving. It will, of course, be a question of balancing the books, investment by a greater number of people and thus more cash floating round the economy against the effect on the chancellor's Tax income.

Financial Strength

You must not forget, however, that rates of performance are not everything, especially if you never see your money again! Accordingly, you must ensure that any organisation with whom you invest has requisite financial strength to still be around tomorrow. The financial services market place is extremely competitive, and it may well be that either through mergers, take-overs, or even failures, the market contracts over coming years.

You should be able to obtain information on banks and publicly quoted building societies from the report and accounts, whilst life assurance companies and Unit Trust groups generally issue some form of statement as to their financial strength.

Newspapers

There will be survey after survey in the money pages of most newspapers. What you need to remember is that these pages are often written with one eye on the potential advertisers. Have you ever seen one advise you not to invest in PEPs? You would think that over 12 years there's be at least one article saying they were 'bad value', even if it were wrong. But no, that would lose valuable advertising income. In short, ask yourself if you should really believe everything you read in the business pages!

Finding an Advisor

If you already have a portfolio or have other savings media, then you may have an advisor. It would be reasonable for you to consult him or her in the first instance to see what their view is. Alternatively, you may be a first time investor, or someone who simply needs a new advisor. If so, you need to re-read *'The Golden Rules of ISA Purchase'* which explains how to find an advisor, not just for the purpose of establishing an ISA, but for any other purpose.

Chapter Twelve

Where To Obtain (More) Information

One of the problems all would-be investors will face, is the difficulty of obtaining accurate and useful information. A simple examination of advertisements and publicity material issued by the current providers of PEPs and TESSAs seems to indicate that they are all fabulous performers and have all beaten one another! Of course, common sense dictates that this cannot be the case, but how do you prove it? This section is intended to point you towards sources of useful information so that you can make an informed choice.

If you studied the chapter which considers how best to obtain your ISA, you will be well on your way. However, even if dealing with a quality financial adviser, or some other trusted source, it would be useful to have backup independent verification of any facts.

The way figures are massaged

Most investment institutions employ an army of people in their marketing and publicity departments. It is their job to take the information provided by the technical people and put it in a format likely to produce more sales. This leads to some rather selective advertising and some fairly unrealistic claims.

The Selective Criteria Method

Imagine you are the manager of a UK share fund which is 50th in the top 100. You obviously need to improve this so you start to examine the 49 above and see how they can be excluded from your list. If your fund is £50 million in size, then you might be justified in excluding anybody whose fund is anymore than twice as big. This should get rid of half of them. Then, you might discover that very few of them have been in existence as long as you, and so you can exclude those who haven't. By carrying on this process and using a very selective definition you can actually get rid of all 49 who are above you and legitimately produce a chart which shows you to be the top!

There was one famous occasion when an investment house claimed to have the best ever Japanese fund but when you read the small print it said "managed by a team of women, based in Osaka not Tokyo, being less than £35 million in size, having existed for less than four years." So sad though it may seem, the long and the short of it is that much of what is produced by the institutions themselves is useful for lighting your fire, and little else.

Unfair Comparisons

Another way of engineering your performance figures to be better than your competitors, is to make unfair comparisons. Imagine, for example, everybody publishes results of their managed funds. These funds would include property and cash as well as shares. If your fund only includes shares, and in the previous few years shares have rocketed up whilst property and cash have stayed constant, then you are bound to outperform them. Of course, there is no need to tell investors that your fund really is not at all comparable with the others, despite the fact you have called it "Managed", when "UK equity", might be more appropriate.

These are just two simple means by which the public can be hoodwinked.

Sources of Accurate Information

Clearly, in order to establish what the truth really is, you will need to obtain some sort of independent information. It is almost impossible to do this, because whoever produces the figures will have some sort of spin which will be reflected in their usefulness. For example, some major firms of actuaries produce pension performance figures, but as those firms of actuaries are involved in pension fund management, then it would be a brave man who deems the figures to be absolutely independent.

Further, some might suggest that the Unit Trust houses producing comparisons of unit and Investment Trusts, would favour Unit Trusts, whilst the Investment Trust organisations would favour themselves over the Unit Trusts.

However, there are some very useful sources of information listed below.

1.   **The Saturday and Sunday Press** – When factual information is being gathered or summarised it can be a useful guide. As long as you do not take any one article as representative, and obtain a variety of different views, you should begin to see a trend.

    For example, if you see a table of top PEPs with Perpetual, Fidelity, Newton and Schroder in it, along with two or three names you don't know, you are likely to continue seeing the four big names in the tables whilst the fringe names change. You should be able to establish a trend.

2.   **The Internet** – there has been an explosion of information on the Internet to the extent that there is probably too much. However, it must be worth an afternoon's browsing if you have access, in order to download data.

3.   **Television and Radio** – the quality of information on television and radio is often largely dictated by the needs of the producer and the format of the show. However, there are a great many serious and sincere researchers providing the underlying facts. These people are rarely the glory seekers in front of the camera and may therefore exhibit higher less-self-seeking levels of journalistic ethics.

4.   **Financial Advisors -** There are two very useful sources of information here. One is information produced in-house by major firms of advisers, and the other is information to which they have access and might be happy to let you see.

   In-house surveys will perhaps have something of a spin, but may nonetheless be generated to satisfy the regulators. Accordingly, the methodology is generally fairly sound.

   As for third party information, the bigger firms of advisors might pay thousands of pounds for independent reports produced by major firms of accountants. If you can have access to this sort of research, then you should be fairly confident that the results you get are accurate.

5.   **Technical Information -** Of course, it is not just investment results which matter, but technical information. There are quite a few pitfalls with the ISA, and unless you have competent advisors or look into matters in great depth yourself, you could fall into one of these traps.

Major fund management groups, banks and insurance companies are likely to check and check again anything they send out. The provisions of the Financial Services Act are so tight that it is unlikely that inaccurate information will be published.

Accordingly, you should be able to trust what you read when it has been produced by a major institution.

Buyer Beware

Of course, "buyer beware" still applies. No matter what information you get or where you get it from, you must not leave your common sense at home. If something seems too good to be true, then it usually is. Anything that worries you should be checked and checked again before you start to apply your hard earned money to any particular scheme.

Useful Organisations

The Personal Investment Authority
1 Canada Square, Canary Wharf, London, E14 5AZ
Telephone 0171 538 8860.
Fax 0171 538 9300

The PIA Ombudsman
3rd Floor, Centre Point, 103 New Oxford Street,
London, WC1A 1QH
Telephone 0171 379 0444.
Fax 0171 240 9500

The Investment Ombudsman
Lloyds Chambers, 1 Portsoken Street, London, E1 8BT,
Telephone 0171 390 5000
Fax 0171 680 0550

The Building Society Ombudsman
Millbank Tower, Millbank, London, SW1P 4XS
Telephone 0171 931 0044.
Fax 0171 931 8484

The Banking Ombudsman
70 Greysend Road, London, WC1X 8NB
Telephone 0171 404 9944
Fax 0171 405 5052

The Occupational Pensions Advisory Service
11 Belgrave Road, London, SW1V 1RB
Telephone 0171 233 8080
Fax 0171 233 8016

The Pensions Ombudsman
11 Belgrave Road, London, SW1V 1RB
Telephone 0171 834 9144
Fax 0171 821 0065

Securities and Investment Board
Greville House, 2/14 Bunhill Row, London, EC1Y 8RA,
Telephone 0171 638 1240
Fax 0171 382 5900

Useful Numbers

_____

_____

_____

_____

_____

_____

_____

Chapter Thirteen

Conclusion

So far you have seen what an ISA is, how it is structured, and what it will do. Further, you have seen how it can be adapted to suit your personal aims, once you have defined them clearly.

You have seen how it can assist in building up deposits for house purchases, and in paying off that mortgage over the years.

You have seen how it can help build up your pension and boost your retirement income, help educate your children, pay for holidays or other personal expenditure.

You should now have an understanding of the tax benefits and the consequences of these in terms of enhancing the investment.

Finally, you should have a clear idea of where to go in order to get yourself an ISA, and how to evaluate its relative competitiveness in terms of charges and likely performance. But for all this, the key issue will be to step back from the ISA itself and consider your own personal needs first. This was made clear at the outset, but unless you consider the ISA and any other financial instrument to be a tool to achieve your clearly defined aims, then not only will it not achieve what the Government set out to achieve, but much more significantly, nor will you.

The Golden Rules for ISA Purchase

1. First of all begin with you – decide exactly what your aims are before even considering an ISA.

2. Don't be in a rush – invest in haste, repent at leisure is an old adage, and if you are pressured into a decision it will generally be the wrong one.

3. Use a jury – obtain information from several different sources before making your decision.

4. Understand the rules – you do not want to be caught out by any of the ISA pitfalls, which will take some years before they are changed. So make sure you understand the rules.

5. Check for regulation – make certain the people who advise you are regulated under the Financial Services Act. This is a simple process and they should provide documentary evidence if you ask.

6. Concentrate on value for money – don't focus just on the charges or the apparent lack of charges with an ISA. Ask yourself what the product really does for you and whether the price is reasonable in your view. It is better to pay a little more for successful investment results, than get bad results cheaply.

7. Remember that it is always your money – if for any reason you are unhappy, you can get it back.

Glossary

Age Allowance
An increased personal allowance for thosepeople aged 65 or over at the beginning of the tax year.

Annuity
A mechanism whereby an accrued pension fund is converted into an income stream usually for policy holders lifetime

Avoidance
The use of legitimate means to reduce your tax bill

Bid and Offer Spread
The difference between buying and selling price of shares or Unit Trusts

Budget
The annual presentations for the House of Commons by the Chancellor of changes in financial policy

Bear Market
A stock market where prices are falling rapidly

Bull Market
Stock markets where prices are moving upwards rapidly

CAT Mark
A standard indication that a particular ISA has met the Government guidelines on cost, access and terms

Cash Component
The cash element which makes up part of a maxi ISA or a Mini ISA

CGT
Capital Gains Tax levied on gains in asset prices on disposal

Derivatives
A fairly complicated investment mechanism to increase the gearing on the effect of price movements in various shares or commodities

Dow Jones Index
An index of major shares traded in the United States

Evasion
Illegal methods used to avoid paying tax

FTSE Index
An index of the top 100 shares by capitalisation traded in the UK market

FT All Share Index
A wider index of prices of shares traded in the UK market

Fund Manager
Individual or team responsible for making the day to day decisions with an investment fund

Independent Advisor
An advisor who is not tied to any particular insurance company, investment house or bank, who should therefore be in a position to make an independent recommendation

IFA
See independent advisor

IMRO
The Investment Management Regulatory Organisation

Indexation Allowance
A process of allowing for inflation on chargeable gains so that only the true gain is taxed

Investment Trust Shares
Shares in a listed company which pools investment to give a greater diversification for shareholders, and of which there is a finite number available.

ISA
The new form of tax shelter capable of holding cash, in-surance products, shares, corporate bonds, gilts or National Savings products, and offering considerable tax benefits.

Maxi ISA
An account which is made up of stocks and shares (with or without a cash component)

Mini ISA
An account which is made up of either stocks and shares or cash but not both

Mutual Life Assurance Co
A life assurance company owned by the policy holders

Nikkei-Dow
An index of shares traded in Japan

OEIC
An Open Ended Investment Company to which many Unit Trusts are now converting

Pension Plan
Scheme intended to build up funds for retirement

Personal Allowances
A set level of deduction from income before income tax is applied

Personal Equity Plan (PEP)
A mechanism for the holding of shares and Unit Trusts on which there would be no income tax or capital gains tax (being phased out in April 1999)

PIA
The Personal Investment Authority which regulates UK investment business.

Pound Cost Averaging
Phenomenon whereby regular purchase of shares can help to iron out the fluctuations in underlying share prices

Real Return
The rate of return on an investment in excess of the prevailing rate of inflation

Risk Banding
Process of creating a variety of different investments, different risk profiles in order to achieve an overall effect

Roll up
Way an account compounds in value over time

Surrender Penalty
Levy imposed on the value of the fund when that fund is moved
to another manager or in cash

TESSA
Tax Exempt Special Savings Arrangement which allowed the
income from a deposit account to be credited without income
tax deduction subject to compliance with the regulations

Tied Agent
An individual who acts on behalf of only one insurance company
or one investment institution and is unable to give independent
financial advice

Tracker Fund
Pooled investment fund which seeks to replicate the
performance of a particular index by purchasing the components
of that index in the relevant proportions

Unit Trust
Pooled investment which is open-ended in that it can continue
to take money indefinitely

With-profit Fund
A diversified investment fund intended to provide a steady rate
of return via the declaration of annual and other bonuses

Year of Assessment
The tax year which runs from April 6th through to April 5th
each year

Appendix

Cash			
NIL	**Income Tax Basic**	**Higher**	**Capital Gains Tax**
▼	▼	▼	▼
Reclaim	No Further	Further	No Tax

National Savings Account			
NIL	**Income Tax Basic**	**Higher**	**Capital Gains Tax**
▼	▼	▼	▼
No Tax	No Tax	No Tax	No Tax

National Savings Inc. Bonds			
NIL	**Income Tax Basic**	**Higher**	**Capital Gains Tax**
▼	▼	▼	▼
No Tax	Basic Rate to Pay	Basic and Higher to Pay	No Tax

Gilts/Corporate Bonds			
NIL	Income Tax Basic	Higher	Capital Gains Tax
Reclaim	No Further	Further	No Tax

National Savings Certificates			
NIL	Income Tax Basic	Higher	Capital Gains Tax
No Tax	No Tax	No Tax	No Tax

Shares			
NIL	Income Tax Basic	Higher	Capital Gains Tax
Reclaim	No Further	Further	Yes

Unit Trusts			
NIL	Income Tax Basic	Higher	Capital Gains Tax
Reclaim	No Further	Further	Yes

Investment Trusts			
NIL	**Income Tax Basic**	**Higher**	**Capital Gains Tax**
Reclaim	No Further	Further	Yes

Insurance Bonds			
NIL	**Income Tax Basic**	**Higher**	**Capital Gains Tax**
No Tax No Reclaim	No Tax	Further	No Tax

Offshore Insurance Bonds			
NIL	**Income Tax Basic**	**Higher**	**Capital Gains Tax**
No Tax	Basic Rate to Pay	Basic and Higher to Pay	No Tax

Individual Savings Account			
NIL	**Income Tax Basic**	**Higher**	**Capital Gains Tax**
No Tax	No Tax	No Tax	No Tax

Venture Capital Trusts			
NIL	Income Tax Basic	Higher	Capital Gains Tax
No Tax	No Tax	No Tax	No Tax

Offshore Roll-Up Funds			
NIL	Income Tax Basic	Higher	Capital Gains Tax
No Tax	Basic Rate to Pay	Basic and Higher to Pay	No Tax

Purchased Life Annuities			
NIL	Income Tax Basic	Higher	Capital Gains Tax
Reclaim	Basic Rate to Pay	Further	No Tax

Pension Income			
NIL	Income Tax Basic	Higher	Capital Gains Tax
Reclaim	No Further	Further	No Tax

2nd Hand Life Policies			
NIL	Income Tax Basic	Higher	Capital Gains Tax
No Tax	No Tax	No Tax	Yes

Qualifying Life Policies			
NIL	Income Tax Basic	Higher	Capital Gains Tax
No Tax	No Tax	No Tax	No Tax

Guaranteed Income Bonds			
NIL	Income Tax Basic	Higher	Capital Gains Tax
No Tax	No Further	Further	No Tax

Notes

_____

_____

_____

_____

_____

Complete Beginner's Guide to the Internet

Everywhere you turn these days, it's Internet this, Cyberspace that and Superhighway the other. Indeed, hardly a day goes by without us being bombarded with information and reasons why you should be on the Net. But none of that is of much help in making an informed decision about joining and using the Internet.

What exactly is The Internet? Where did it come from and where is it going? And, more importantly, how can everybody take their place in this new community? *The Complete Beginner's Guide to The Internet* answers all of those questions and more. On top of being an indispensable guide to the basics of Cyberspace, it is the lowest priced introduction on the market by a long way. £5.95

Find What You Want on The Internet

The sheer size of the Internet's information resources is its biggest challenge. There is no central repository of all this information, nor it is catalogued or sorted in ordered fashion.

Find What You Want on The Internet is designed to teach Internet users - from novices to veterans - how to locate information quickly and easily. The book uses jargon-free language, combined with many illustrations, to answer such questions as:

❑ Which search techniques and Search Engines work best for your specific needs?
❑ What is the real difference between true 'search' sites and on-line directories, and how do you decide which one to use?
❑ How do the most powerful Search Engines really work?
❑ Are there any 'special tricks' that will help you find what you want, faster?

There is also a bonus chapter covering Intelligent Agents

£5.95

Investing on the Internet

The world of investment is a dangerous place. No matter how independent your financial advisor claims to be, they always seem to sell you a 'product' with the highest commission to them; witness the pensions scandal of the 80s and early 90s. Even if you receive good advice, there is a huge slab of commission to be paid.

That is why many investors are turning to the Internet. There, they are able to research companies in depth, examine price movements, discuss the merits with other investors and finally invest their money with very service low charges (due to the automation of the process).

Finding exactly what you want on the Internet is extremely difficult. There are several hundred million sites already in existence, and an estimated six million new pages are being added every week. Unfortunately there is no central repository for information and no catalogue of web sites. As a result, searching for the pages you want to view is a time consuming task, and frustrating when irrelevant pages and bad hits get in your way.

INVESTING on the Internet provides a detailed listing of the best sites in this category. Each site is reviewed in terms of content, layout and design, as well as the technical aspects such as speed of downloading, size of graphics and ease of internal navigation.

£4.95

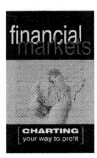

Timing The Financial Markets: Charting Your Way to Profit

Timing The Financial Markets shows all levels of investors, step-by-step, how to construct charts and graphs of price movements for bonds, shares and commodities. Then it explains, in easy-to-understand language, how to interpret the results and turn them into profit.   £6.95

Understand Shares in a Day

Shows how the share market really works. Inexperienced investors will learn: ❑ About different types of shares ...❑ Why share prices fluctuate... ❑ How to read the financial pages ...❑ How shares are bought and sold ...❑ How risk can be spread with investment and unit trusts ... ❑ How to build a portfolio of shares ...❑ The risks and rewards associated with Penny Shares

Once this basic groundwork has been covered, the book explores more complex ideas which will appeal to both beginners and more experienced investors alike, including: ● How to value shares ● How equity options are used by professional investors to 'gear' profits and hedge against falling share prices. £6.95

Understand Bonds & Gilts in a Day

This handy title shows potential investors, and those with an interest in the bond markets, how to assess the potential risks and rewards, giving a simple to follow set of criteria on which to base investment decisions. Having shown the inexperienced investor how to go about buying bonds, it also teaches even the most arithmetically shy how to calculate the yield on a bond and plan an income based portfolio. The confusing terminology used in the bond market is clearly explained with working definitions of many terms and a comprehensive glossary. £6.95

Tax Self-Assessment Made Easy

The book tells you what you have to do and when to do it, warning you of what happens if you don't. Chapters include:
● Self-employed and the effects... ● Directors and trustees...
● Record keeping requirements ● Penalties and surcharges...
● People on PAYE ... ● What companies need to do... etc...
An essential guide with schedules to help you ensure that your tax bill is correct in the first place. £6.95

ISAs Made Easy

Understand Derivatives in a Day

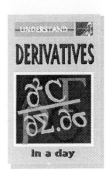

Financial derivatives are used as highly-geared vehicles for making money, saving money or preventing its loss. They also have the ability to exploit volatility, guarantee results and avoid taxes. But only if they are used correctly.

Learn...How private investors get started... To Hedge, Straddle and control Risk... Ways to limit the downside but not the upside... About risk free derivative strategies... Trading Psychology - Fear, Hope and Greed... Also, the History of Derivatives; Currency Speculation; Long and Short puts; Tarantula Trading; and much more. £6.95

Understand Financial Risk in a Day

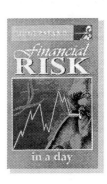

Risk management is all about minimising risks and maximising opportunities. Those who understand what they should be doing, as a result of their risk calculations, will usually come out as winners. Those who flail in the dark will, more often than not, be the losers.

Understand Financial Risk in a Day is a perfect introduction to the subject. Light on detailed formulae and heavy on easy-to-follow examples it will lead the reader to a greater awareness of how to evaluate the risks they are facing and adapt a strategy to create the best possible outcome. £6.95

The International Dictionary of Personal Finance

This dictionary provides a basic vocabulary of terms used in the world of personal finance, from 'A' shares to zero-rating and from accelerated depreciation to yield. examples of usage, and linked to other terms in the book. £6.95

Book Ordering

Please complete the form below or use a plain piece of paper and send to:

Europe/Asia

TTL, PO Box 200, Harrogate HG1 2YR, England (or fax to 01423-526035, or email: sales@net-works.co.uk).

USA/Canada

Trafalgar Square, PO Box 257, Howe Hill Road, North Pomfret, Vermont 05053 (or fax to 802-457-1913, call toll free 800-423-4525, or email: tsquare@sover.net)

Postage and handling charge:

UK - £1 for first book, and 50p for each additional book

USA - $5 for first book, and $2 for each additional book (all shipments by UPS, please provide street address).

Elsewhere - £3 for first book, and £1.50 for each additional book via surface post (for airmail and courier rates, please fax or email for a price quote)

Book	Qty	Price

❑ I enclose payment for _____

Postage

Total:

❑ Please debit my Visa/Amex/Mastercard No:

Expiry date: [ ][ ][ ][ ]   Signature:

Name: _____

Address: _____

_____

_____

Postcode/Zip: _____

ISAbook